The microscope is a very important tool of science. Read page 5 to discover who first used a microscope to observe tiny creatures.

Learn about gene therapy on page 10 and decide how you feel about the advantages and disadvantages of this new technology.

Read **Scientists Crack the Human Code!** on page 11 to learn about the completion of the Human Genome Project.

Discover new technology in **Artificial Red Blood Cells** on page 27 that could help you to run for 15 minutes without taking a single breath.

What is genetic engineering?

Visit www.infosteps.co.uk
for more about THE INVISIBLE WORLD.

More Than Meets the Eye

An Invisible World

The power of the human eye is incredible. If you look around you can see different objects, shapes, sizes and a huge range of colours. At night you can see a star shining as far away as another galaxy. At the beach you can see tiny grains of sand. But even if you have perfect eyesight anything less than 0.1 millimetres—the size of a pinpoint—disappears into a world you can no longer see with your eyes alone, an invisible world!

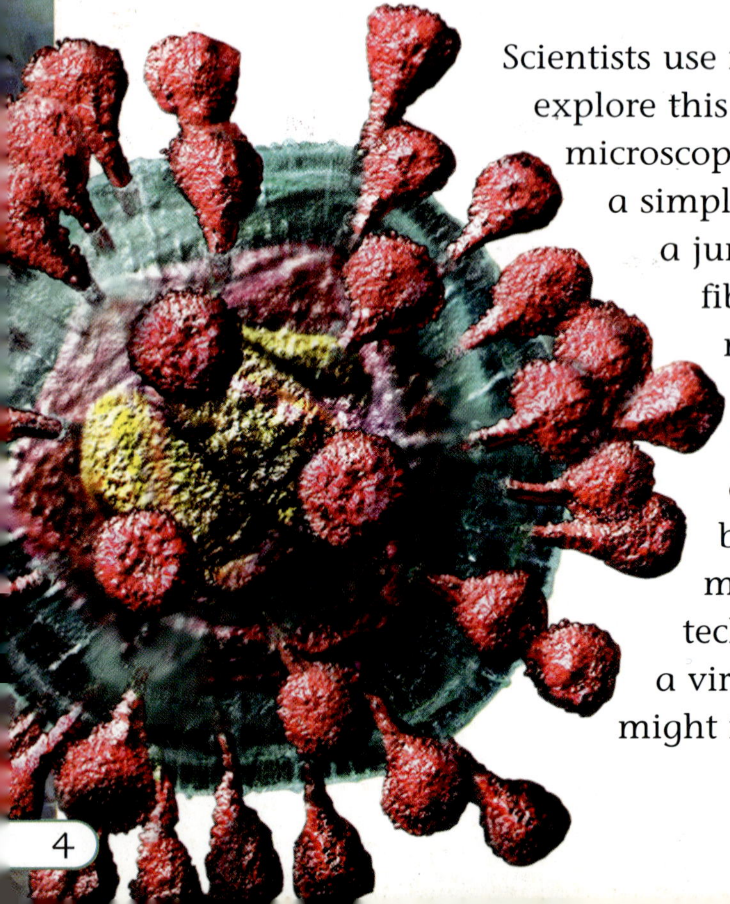

Scientists use microscopes to explore this tiny realm. A microscope can transform a simple dust ball into a jungle of hairs and fibres alive with microscopic creatures. It can magnify tissue to show the workings of a cell. It can also be used to build tiny machines to advance technology or to identify a virus (shown left) that might invade a healthy cell.

Anton van Leeuwenhoek (1632–1723)

Anton van Leeuwenhoek was the first scientist to use a microscope. He worked as a cloth merchant in the Netherlands and built his own simple microscopes to help test the quality of his cloth. Leeuwenhoek was fascinated by the tiny animals he saw moving on the cloth under his microscope. He called these **micro-organisms** animalcules. Leeuwenhoek was the first person to study and document this invisible world. He described red blood cells and bacteria and he showed how sap moved through a plant. With his discovery of animalcules Leeuwenhoek revolutionized biology.

Magnificent Microscopes

Scientists use light microscopes and electron microscopes to magnify **specimens**. They study details of cells, bacteria, insects, viruses and many other micro-organisms and objects too small to see with the naked eye.

A light microscope works by shining light onto a specimen. The light bounces off the object and glass lenses bend the light to form a magnified image. A light microscope can only show details that are large enough to bend light rays.

Electron microscopes use electron beams instead of light beams and can magnify many more times than light microscopes. There are two different types of electron microscopes. A transmission electron microscope, or TEM, fires a beam of electrons through a specimen. It can only shoot electrons through a very thin flat slice of material, so it cannot be used to view large living specimens. When scientists want to look at three-dimensional images they use a scanning electron microscope, or SEM. The specimen must first be coated with a film of metal atoms. Then a beam of electrons is used to scan the surface of the specimen. Electrons bounce off the film and transmit the information back to a computer.

This image from a scanning electron microscope shows tiny mites crawling on a cricket.

DNA: A Recipe for Life

Building Blocks

All living things are made up of cells. Each living thing is different because it has its own genetic code, or DNA. Your DNA can be found in the nucleus of every cell in your body. DNA is the control centre with all of the instructions for building your body and telling it how to work. Sections of your DNA are called genes. These tell your cells to make certain **proteins**. A gene may code for a protein that makes your eyes green or your hair curly.

DNA is an acronym for deoxyribonucleic acid.

DNA	
	DEOXY: Being without oxygen
	RIBO: A type of sugar
	NUCLEIC: In the nucleus of a cell
	ACID: A sour chemical

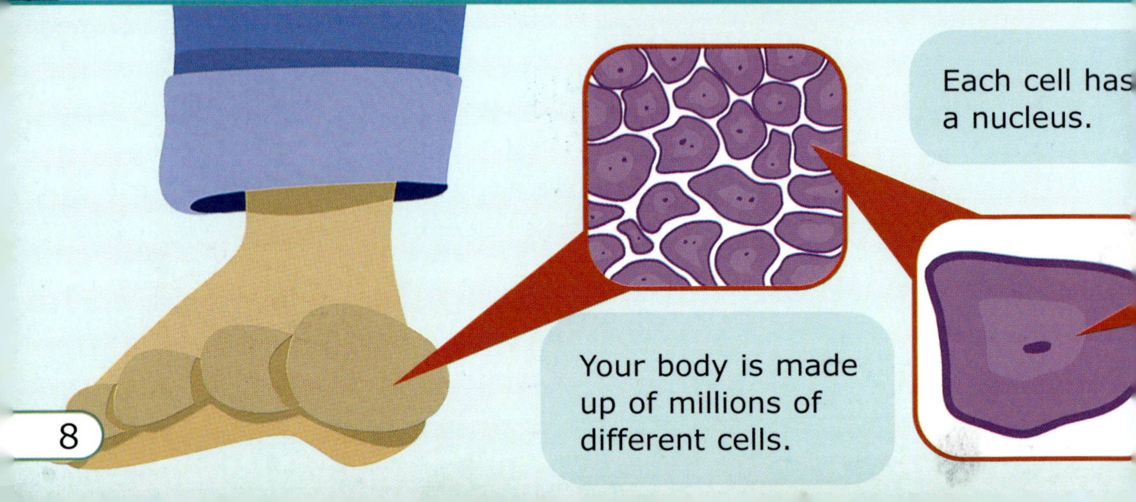

Watson and Crick

DNA is so small that it can't even be seen under a microscope. On February 28, 1953 James Watson and Francis Crick unveiled an amazing discovery. They worked out and built a model showing the structure of DNA. They discovered that DNA is shaped like a twisted ladder, called a double helix. This sparked a scientific revolution and helped other scientists to discover how DNA works and makes copies of itself before a cell divides. In 1962 Watson, Crick and their partner Maurice Wilkins won the Nobel Prize for their extraordinary work.

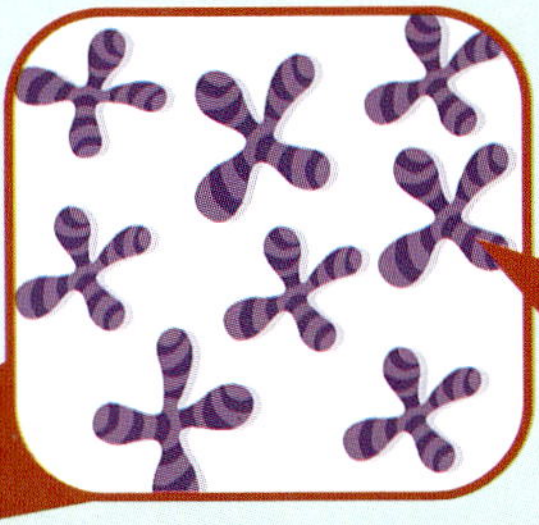

Inside the nucleus is a collection of 46 chromosomes.

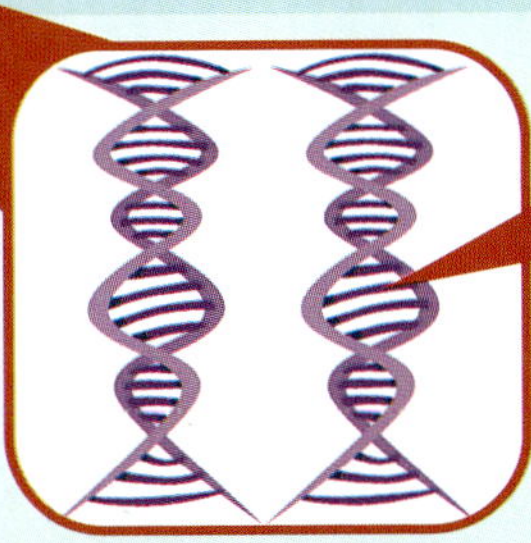

Each chromosome is made up of two tightly wound spirals of DNA.

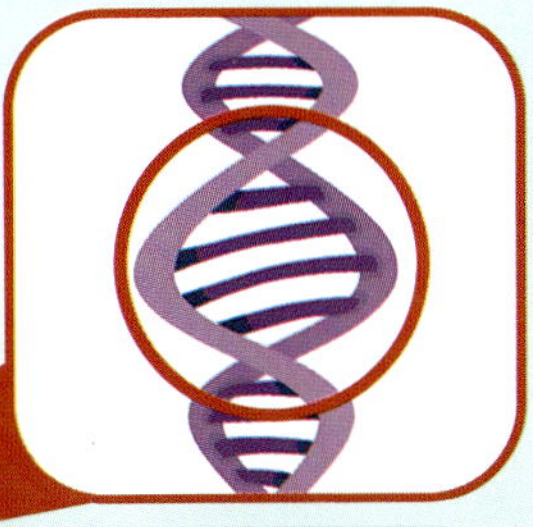

Genes are sections, or pieces, of DNA.

The Gene Scene

DNA is not perfect. Mutations, or changes in the genetic code, can occur. Some mutations are good because they can help plants and animals adapt to changes in their environments. But some mutations are bad because they can cause illness or sometimes even death.

WHAT'S YOUR OPINION?

Scientists are working on ways to fix faulty genes. This is called gene therapy. Having a greater understanding of their genetic make-up can help people to find out early if they have faulty genes so they can get medical help before they get sick. There is a risk, however, that individuals would have to give genetic information to other people such as employers and insurance companies. There is also a possibility that people with faulty genes may choose not to have children. Do you think it's a good idea or a bad idea for people to know if they have faulty genes?

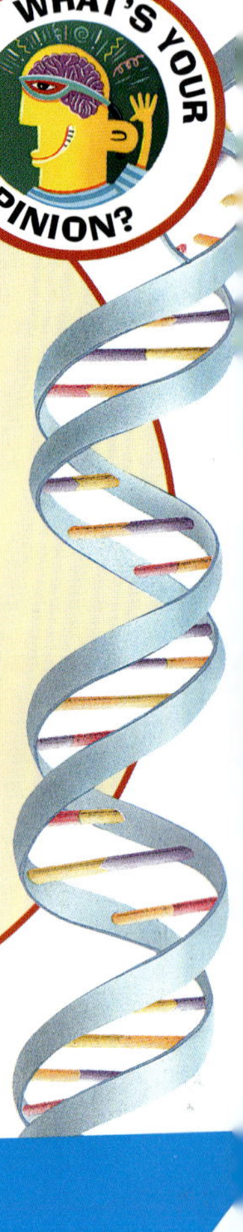

SITESEEING • SCIENCE & TECHNOLOGY •

What is genetic engineering?

Visit www.infosteps.co.uk for more about THE INVISIBLE WORLD.

IN THE NEWS

April 14, 2003

Scientists Crack the Human Code!

A report on the complete sequence of human DNA was released today in Washington, DC. Thousands of scientists in labs around the world have been working to complete the Human **Genome** Project. It has taken over a decade to work out the order of the 3 billion base pairs in the human genetic code. The working report draft was released in 2001 and showed that humans have around 30,000 genes, fewer than scientists had first thought. It also showed that every person on Earth has 99.9% of the same DNA coding as other people. The knowledge of the human genome will help scientists to discover what causes some diseases such as diabetes and cancer. It will make it easier for doctors to diagnose and maybe even prevent some illnesses.

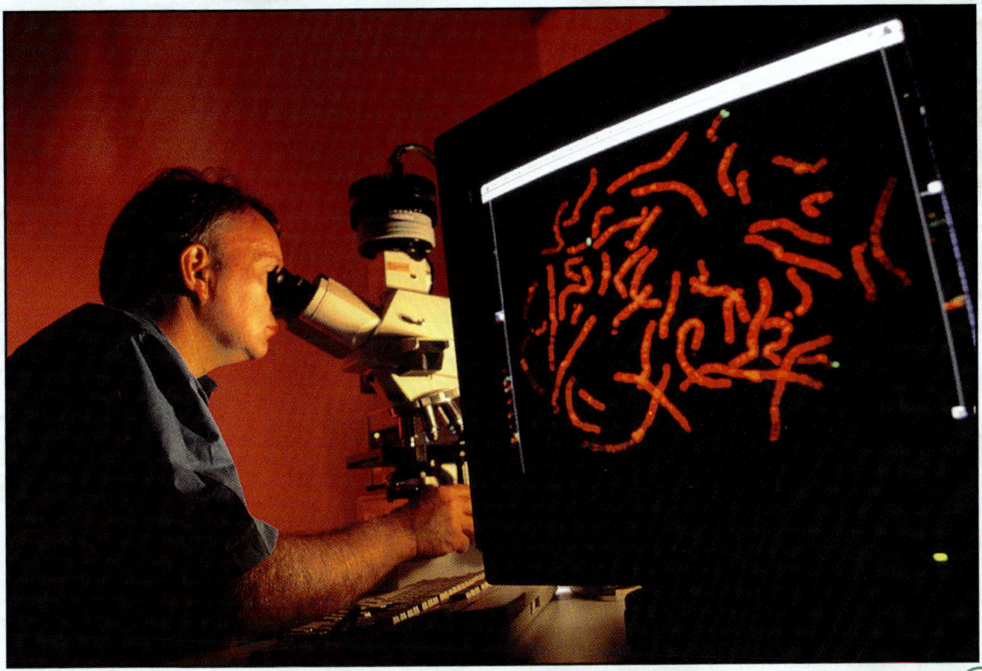

A scientist studying chromosomes for the Human Genome Project.

Innocent or Guilty?

Invisible evidence hidden at a crime scene can match a suspect to a crime or prove that the suspect is innocent. **Forensic scientists** collect evidence and piece together clues to solve mysteries.

The Crime: *Sandy's lunch is missing from her school bag.*

Your Job: *Find the thief!*

Check for Fingerprints

Everybody's fingerprints are unique. If a thief touches something at a crime scene invisible oily sweaty fingerprints are left behind. A fine aluminium dusting powder can be brushed over places where prints might be. The powder is trapped in the sticky sweat and shows the prints. These can be photographed or stuck onto a piece of adhesive tape and taken back to the lab. They are then compared with a suspect's fingerprints.

Your Case:

Two fingerprints were found at the scene. One fingerprint is Sandy's and the other is her best friend's.

Sandy with her best friend, Jane

Sandy's fingerprint

Jane's fingerprint

Analyze the DNA

Everybody has a unique genetic code, so if you find a body cell, you also find a complete set of DNA that can be matched to a person. This code can be found in almost anything left at a scene from the thief's body such as skin cells, blood, hair follicles or saliva.

DNA profiling, or genetic fingerprinting, was developed in the 1980s. Forensic scientists open the cells and let out the long threads of DNA. They then break these into smaller fragments and place them in a special jelly. When an electric current is passed through the jelly the pieces of DNA move and separate into bands according to the size of the fragment. The pattern can be matched to a person's pattern.

Sandy's school bag

Skin cells found on Sandy's school bag

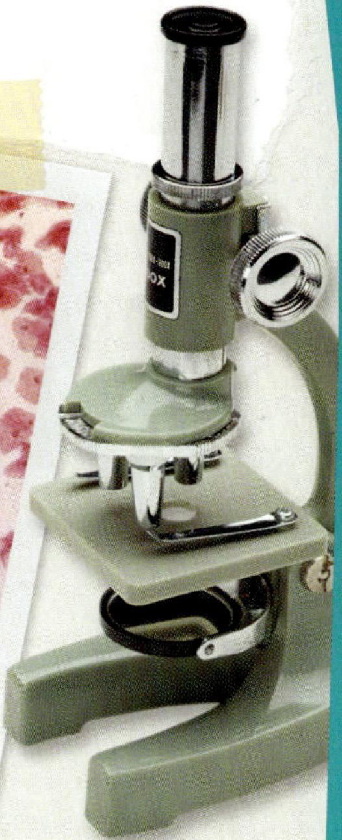

Your Case:

Some skin cells were found. There is no match at this stage. Jane has an alibi. She was at a music lesson. Her DNA was tested and it doesn't match the cells found at the scene. Jane is no longer a suspect.

Check for Other Evidence

Many seeds and pollen can be traced back to specific plants. Seeds from some plants are found only in certain places and at certain times of the year. Bacteria from soil can also be different in different areas and traces of chemicals can help identify the scene of a crime.

Your Case:

Pollen has been found near and on Sandy's bag. The pollen matches the lilies outside Sandy's classroom. You interview the caretaker. He claims he was gardening this morning. His dog, Patch, was with him.

Pollen

Hairs and Fibres

Hairs and fibres are often left behind at a crime scene. Under a microscope these can be matched to a suspect. Animal hairs are different from human hairs.

Your Case:

Several hairs were found. They belong to an animal.

Guilty!

Match:

The DNA from the skin cells match a sample taken from Patch. The hair found at the scene matches Patch's fur which also has pollen on it.

Case Closed

Bacteria Everywhere

Bacteria are some of the smallest living things, but they're also the most abundant form of life on Earth—they're everywhere! A single drop of water may contain hundreds of millions of these single-celled organisms. Billions of bacteria make their home on and inside your body. In fact these bacteria outnumber your body's own cells! While some bacteria can be harmful many others can be helpful or even vital for survival.

Open Wide!

Your mouth is an excellent place for bacteria to live and grow—it's warm, moist and there's a good supply of food! Bacteria have plenty of places to live: on your tongue, teeth, gums or the linings of your cheeks. These bacteria live in balance alongside other micro-organisms. As long as they all continue to live in balance you will have a very healthy mouth!

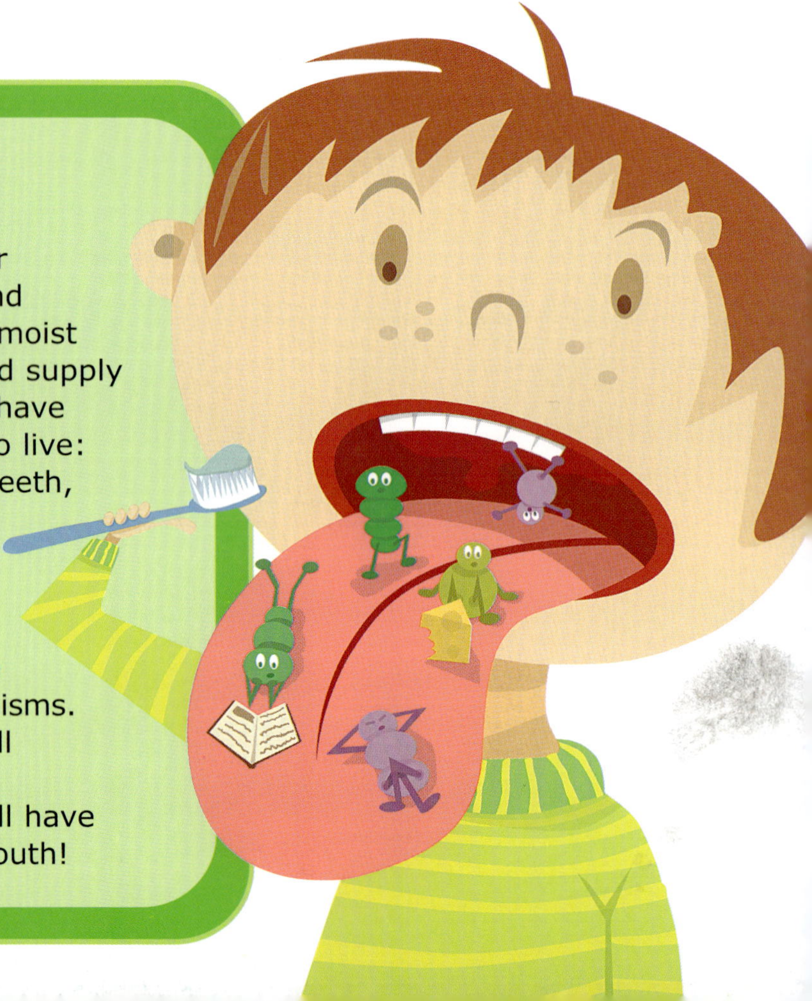

IN FOCUS

Don't Wash Your T-Shirt—Feed It!

Scientist Alex Fowler has been researching ways to make clothes crawl with bacteria. A type of helpful bacteria put into each fibre of a fabric could act as a cleaner by eating the chemicals that make dirty clothes smell bad.

Q. Dr Fowler, how do you get the bacteria into the fabric?

A. One way is to load the bacteria into hollow milkweed fibres. To do this we put the fibres in a vacuum and cover them with a liquid that contains the bacteria. When the vacuum is released the pressure pushes the bacteria into the fibres. These fibres can then be used to make fabrics.

Q. How would the bacteria live in my clothes?

A. While some bacteria might live solely by feeding on your sweat others might need special food. They also might need special soap. Some scientists are looking at ways to make "soaps" that would clean your shirt and feed your bacteria at the same time!

Q. Could the bacteria hurt me?

A. The bacteria we use are harmless.

Q. Are there other possible uses for bacteria in fabrics?

A. Some bacteria can glow in the dark and could be used to make fabrics that glow. Some produce chemicals to help heal people. These could be useful for making antiseptic bandages. Some make chemicals that are water-resistant, too. Maybe one day bacteria might even be used to repair torn fabrics!

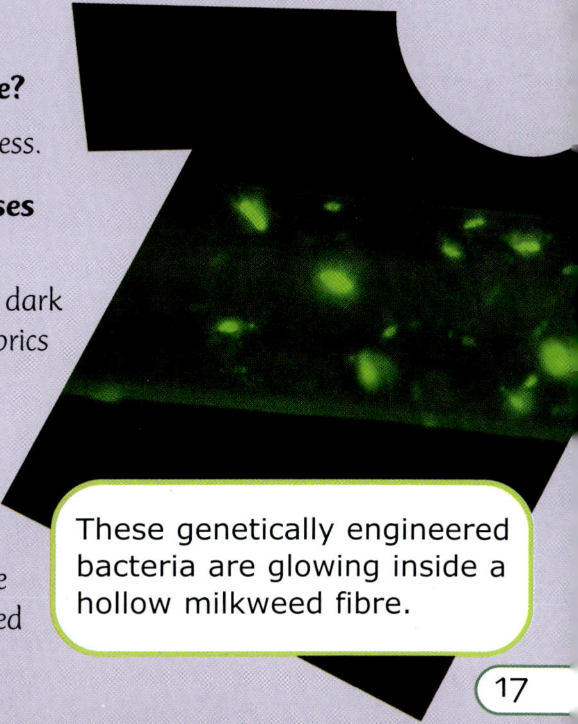

These genetically engineered bacteria are glowing inside a hollow milkweed fibre.

Virus Alert!

Viruses are very simple microscopic organisms that live inside the cells of other living things. They are one of the biggest threats to humans, causing diseases such as mumps, measles, chicken pox and the common cold. They also attack animals, plants and bacteria.

Viruses are simply a collection of nucleic acid, either DNA or **RNA**, coated in a protein capsule. All viruses must find a host cell in which they can **replicate** and grow. They cannot live alone! Viruses invade a healthy cell and transfer their nucleic acid into it. The host cell reads and obeys the virus's genetic code which tells it to make hundreds of copies of the virus. This eventually damages or kills the host cell.

A Basic Viral Cycle

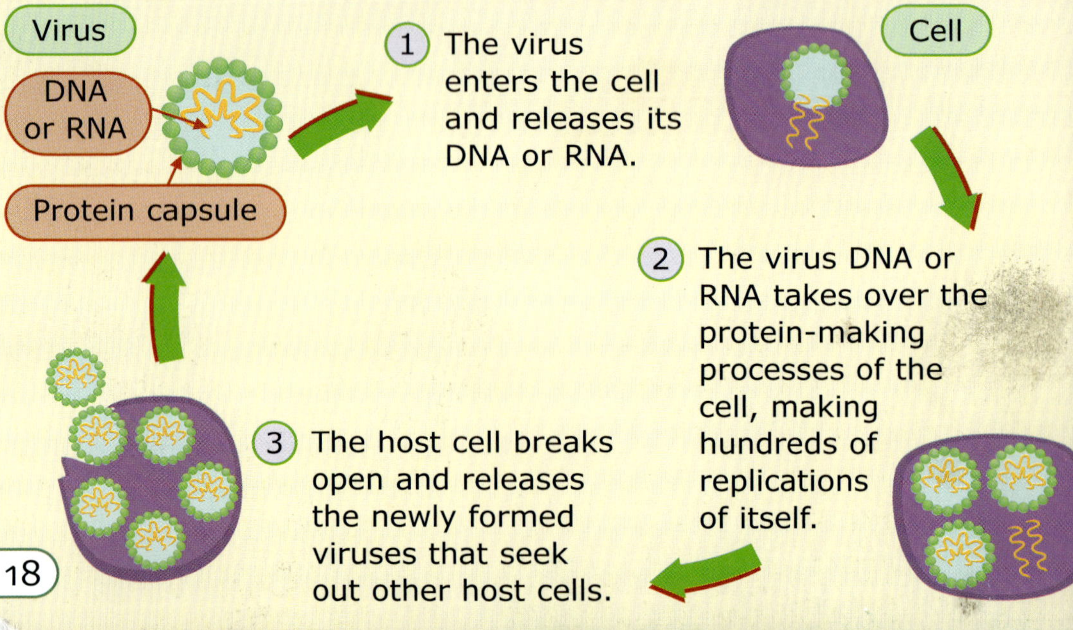

Lymphocytes are cells in the immune system. They help to protect you from viruses in two ways. Some lymphocytes make microscopic defenders called antibodies that attack the protein capsule of a virus and stop it from attaching to a healthy cell. Other lymphocytes destroy cells that have been infected by viruses, killing the viruses before they can multiply.

There are over 100 different viruses that can cause a common cold. These viruses enter your body when you breathe and they target cells in your nose, throat and lungs.

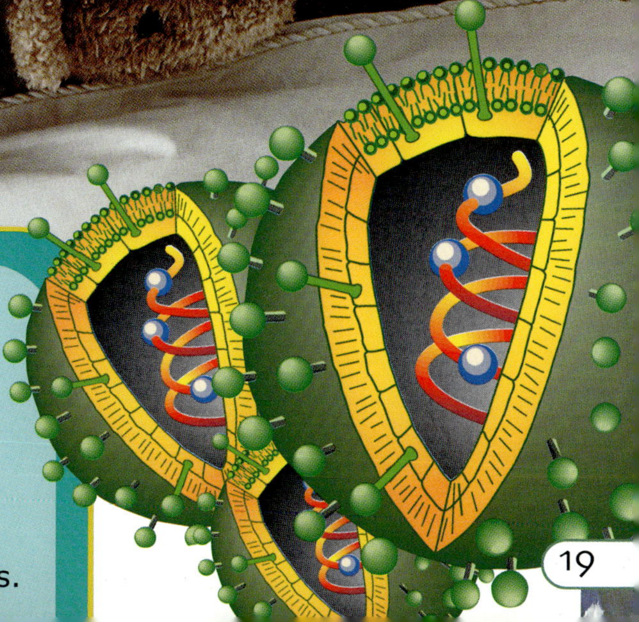

People who study viruses are called virologists. They research how viruses cause diseases so they can create ways to control them. They also use viruses to control insect pests, perform cell research and develop vaccines.

The Mighty Mite

Mites are tiny animals that can live just about anywhere. There are many different kinds of mites. Some are parasites and feed on the blood of animals. Some mites burrow into the skin of people and animals, causing an itchy rash. Others live in the soil and help break down dead plant and animal tissues.

Follicle Mites

You probably have mites right under your nose! Follicle mites thrive in the small hairs on your upper lip, on your eyelashes and in your ears.

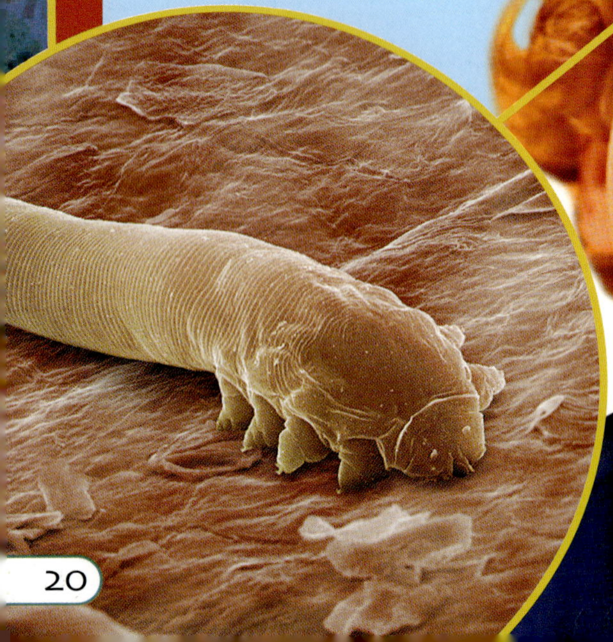

Dust mites live in dust balls that may collect on furniture, gather behind doors or be sucked up by a vacuum cleaner. These dust balls are a microscopic ecosystem full of plant, mineral and animal debris. Dust mites search through a jungle of matted hairs and clothing fibres for dead skin cells to feed on. These mites are so small that up to 5,000 of them can live in a single gram of dust.

Dust Mites

It doesn't matter how clean your home is there will still be millions of dust mites living in carpets, mattresses and other furnishings. For some people these microscopic residents can cause allergies and asthma.

Micro Detective

Q. How can flies see so well?

A. A fly has two large compound eyes that are made up of several thousand eyelets. These cover most of the fly's head. The fly's brain combines the signals from the eyelets to make up an image of its surroundings. The fly doesn't have sharp vision, but it can detect movement very quickly.

Q. How can geckos walk upside down and stick to slippery surfaces?

A. A gecko holds on using two million microscopic hairs, or setae, on its toes. At the tip of each hair are thousands of tiny pads. The molecules on these pads interact with molecules on a surface, sticking the gecko to the surface. This adhesive power is so strong that a million setae, which could easily fit into the area of your thumbnail, could lift a 20-kilogram dog! Scientists are working on a new material that mimics the hairs found on geckos' toes. With this material people may also be able to walk up walls and upside down on ceilings!

Q. Why is my bread green?

A. Mould is a type of fungus that often grows on food. It produces spores that are carried on air currents. When a mould spore settles on food it begins to grow. Most mouldy foods should not be eaten, but a few foods such as blue cheese rely on mould for their taste.

Q. What's special about a cat's tongue?

A. A cat uses its tongue to clean its fur. The surface of its tongue is covered with tiny spikes that act like a comb to clean away dirt and fleas. The spikes also help the cat to lap up water and milk.

Tiny Technology

The Microchip

Machines run by tiny devices play an important role in many people's lives. In 1959 the silicon chip was invented. This led to the creation of the microchip, a piece of silicon crystal with hundreds of thousands of microscopically small electrical components on it. When a microchip is used in a machine it is connected to wires that carry electrical signals. Its job is to either process or store the signals in its memory. The microchip is a common part of many machines, including computers and CD players.

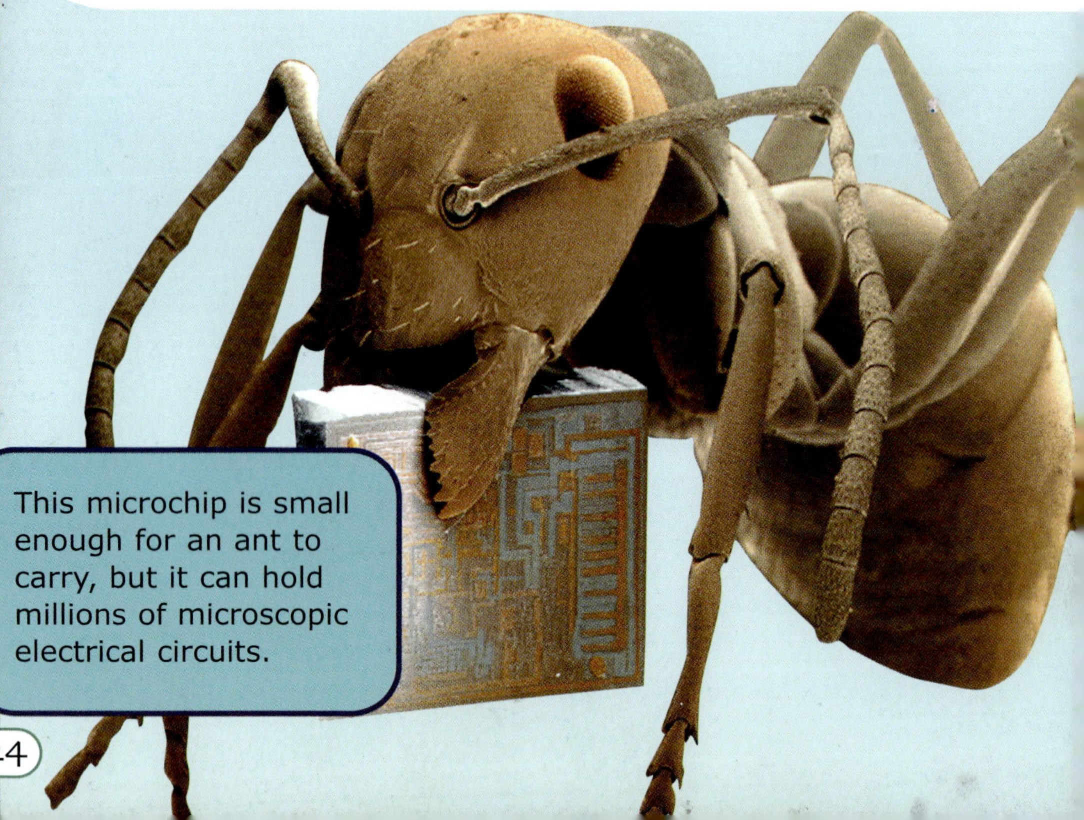

This microchip is small enough for an ant to carry, but it can hold millions of microscopic electrical circuits.

As we rely on microchips to carry more information scientists keep working to make them smaller. Circuits, however, can't keep shrinking forever! Scientists are researching ways to get rid of the metal wires and replace them with light beams. These light beams are much thinner than metal wires, so many more can fit on a chip and send much more information.

Technicians make hundreds of microchips at the same time on silicon wafers. After the wafers have been processed they are divided into single microchips. Technicians wear protective clothing to prevent **contamination** of the wafers.

Nanotechnology

Technology is constantly changing and scientists are always looking for new ways to make technology products smaller and more powerful. Nanotechnology is the science of building tiny microscopic machines atom by atom. These nanomachines would be so small that enough material to build 10,000 of them could fit into a single grain of sand! Scientists believe that these tiny machines would have many uses: they might fix microscopic circuits, be miniature "eyes" that might give some blind people the ability to see or replace passwords as security devices for computers.

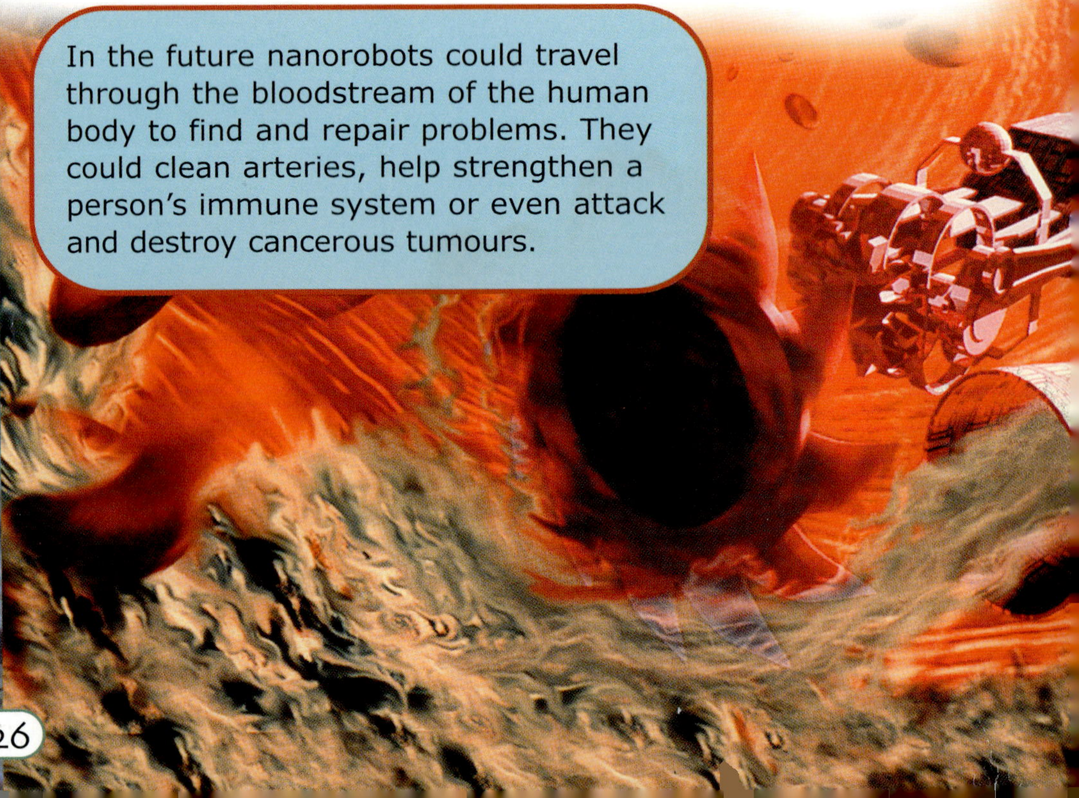

In the future nanorobots could travel through the bloodstream of the human body to find and repair problems. They could clean arteries, help strengthen a person's immune system or even attack and destroy cancerous tumours.

Artificial Red Blood Cells

Scientist Robert Freitas has designed an artificial red blood cell. This tiny machine has small pressure tanks that can carry and store oxygen and carbon dioxide. If an army of these cells was injected into a person's bloodstream they could carry oxygen around the body in the same way real red blood cells do, but 200 times more efficiently! With these artificial cells in your bloodstream you could sit at the bottom of a swimming pool for four hours without breathing or run for 15 minutes without taking a breath.

Fibres and Fabrics

Fibres are long thin hairlike strands that can be spun into yarn and then made into fabrics for items such as clothes, carpets and upholstery. There are two different kinds of fibres. Natural fibres such as cotton, silk or wood come from plants and animals. Manufactured fibres are made from chemicals. The **properties** of a particular fibre depend on its physical structure and chemical make-up.

Killer Clothes

Scientist Robert Engel has developed tiny molecular daggers that can be attached to fabric fibres and "stab" bacteria, fungal spores or other micro-organisms. These molecular daggers can be used to make special clothes such as socks that attack the fungus causing athlete's foot and military uniforms that could kill anthrax. The microbes are chemically attracted to the molecular daggers. The daggers then pierce the microbes, killing them before they can reach you!

Nylon fibres were the first manufactured fibres. They are smooth so liquid slides off easily. Nylon is good for raincoats, umbrellas and tents.

Wool fibres are thick and can trap air to keep you warm. Wool comes from sheep and other animals.

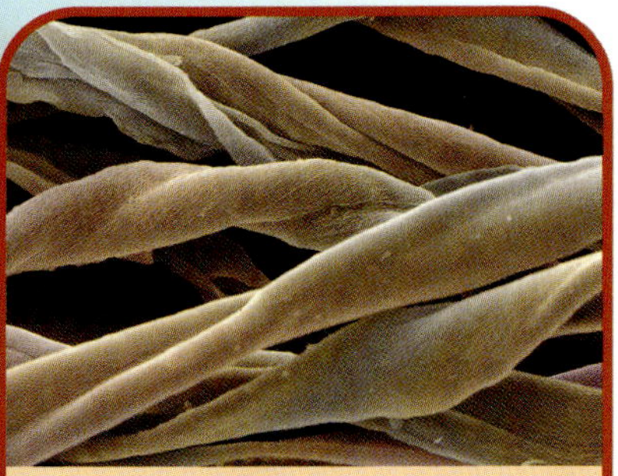

Cotton fibres hold moisture close to your skin. This keeps you cool. Cotton is a natural fibre that comes from a plant.

Glossary

contaminate – to make something dirty

electron – a microscopic particle that moves around the nucleus of an atom

forensic scientist – a scientist who applies scientific knowledge, techniques and methods to the investigation of a crime

genome – all of an organism's genes

micro-organism – a tiny microscopic living being. Bacteria, fungi and viruses are micro-organisms.

property – a characteristic or quality of something

protein – a complex substance made up of nitrogen and other elements. Proteins are very important and are found in all living things.

replicate – to make an exact copy. A virus can make many replications of itself.

RNA – ribonucleic acid. A type of nucleic acid in all living cells. RNA is usually a messenger that carries instructions from DNA to make proteins. In some viruses the genetic information is stored in RNA instead of DNA.

specimen – a small amount of something that is used for testing, study or examination

Index

Bibliography

Applin, David. *Science & You*. Reed Educational and Professional Publishing Limited, 2001.

Burnie, David. *Microlife: An Extraordinary Look from the Inside Out*. Dorling Kindersley, 1997.

Canault, Nina. *Incredibly Small*. Macmillan Publishing Company, 1992.

Graham, Ian. *Crime-Fighting*. Evans, 1993.

Kunkel, Dennis and Howard Tomb. *Microaliens: Dazzling Journeys with an Electron Microscope*. Farrar, Straus and Giroux, 1993.

Research Starters

1 Scientists around the world are constantly making discoveries and thinking of new scientific theories to test. Read newspapers or search the Internet to find out about a recent scientific discovery.

2 You have millions of different bacteria living on and inside your body. Find out about some of these bacteria and whether they are helpful or harmful.

3 Imagine you are a micro detective. Write questions about the micro world like the ones on pages 22–23. Then find the answers to your questions and make drawings of the subjects' microscopic features.

4 Sherlock Holmes has been honoured by the Royal Society of Chemistry for being the first detective to use chemical science to solve crimes. Author Sir Arthur Conan Doyle created Sherlock Holmes as a fictional character over 120 years ago. Read to research great detectives, either fictional or real, and their crime-solving methods.